FROM THE LIBRARY OF

Painting © John Ruthven

B325

This edition published in 1992 by Rainbow Books,
Elsley House, 24–30 Great Titchfield Street, London W1P 7AD

Originally published in 1988 as *Animal Life Stories: The Otter* by Kingfisher Books.

© Grisewood & Dempsey Ltd 1988.

ISBN 1 871745 70 5

End papers by Maurice Pledger.

Printed and bound in Spain.

EYE-VIEW LIBRARY

THE OTTER

By Angela Royston

Illustrated by Bernard Robinson

RAINBOW
· BOOKS ·

It is autumn and moonlight makes the world look silver. The otter is hiding in the dark reeds to eat her fish. A duck is sleeping nearby. Only the little water vole saw the otter slide into the river and dive to catch her meal.

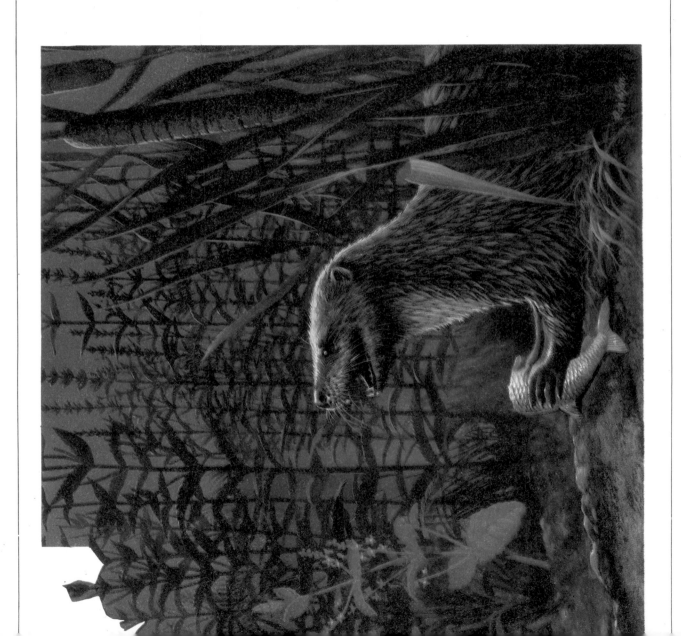

By dawn the otter has finished hunting. She finds a hole in the river bank and squeezes into it. She will sleep all day in this dark, safe tunnel. She lives alone, finding a new hole to sleep in each day.

All through the autumn the otter travels along the river looking for food. She likes to eat fish and crayfish, but sometimes she searches among the reeds for small birds or frogs.

When winter comes the river is covered with a roof of ice. The otter knows that eels and other fish are still swimming beneath it. She breaks a hole in the ice. Taking a deep breath she dives down to hunt.

One night the ice is too thick for the otter to break.
She must find a bigger river where there will be no
ice. She sets off across silent fields covered in deep
snow. She reaches the top of a high hill. Far below,
she sees a river where the water flows freely.

Racing downhill the otter flings herself onto her stomach. Faster and faster she slides, straight down the slippery river bank and into the water.

But soon this river may freeze over too. Night after night she travels downstream towards the warmer sea. She catches fish and eels to eat on the way. Slowly the river widens and the water begins to taste salty like the ocean.

At last the otter reaches the sea. Everything is new and smells strange. She finds shrimps, mussels and small sea fish to eat, but there are no dark holes to sleep in during the day. She longs for fresh water and the comfortable river bank, and so, after a few days, she swims back up the river.

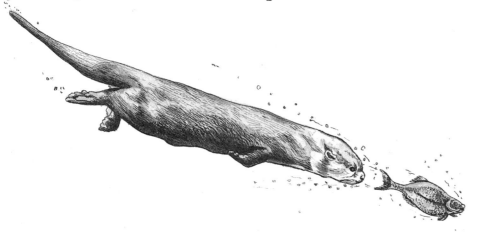

All this time the otter has lived on her own, but one evening on her way upstream she meets another otter, a male. Soon they are playing together. They race along the river bank and dive in and out of the water, chasing fish and ducks.

In the morning the otters each find a separate hole to sleep in, but every night they play and hunt together for frogs and fish. They roll around on the river bank and chase each other, and they become mates.

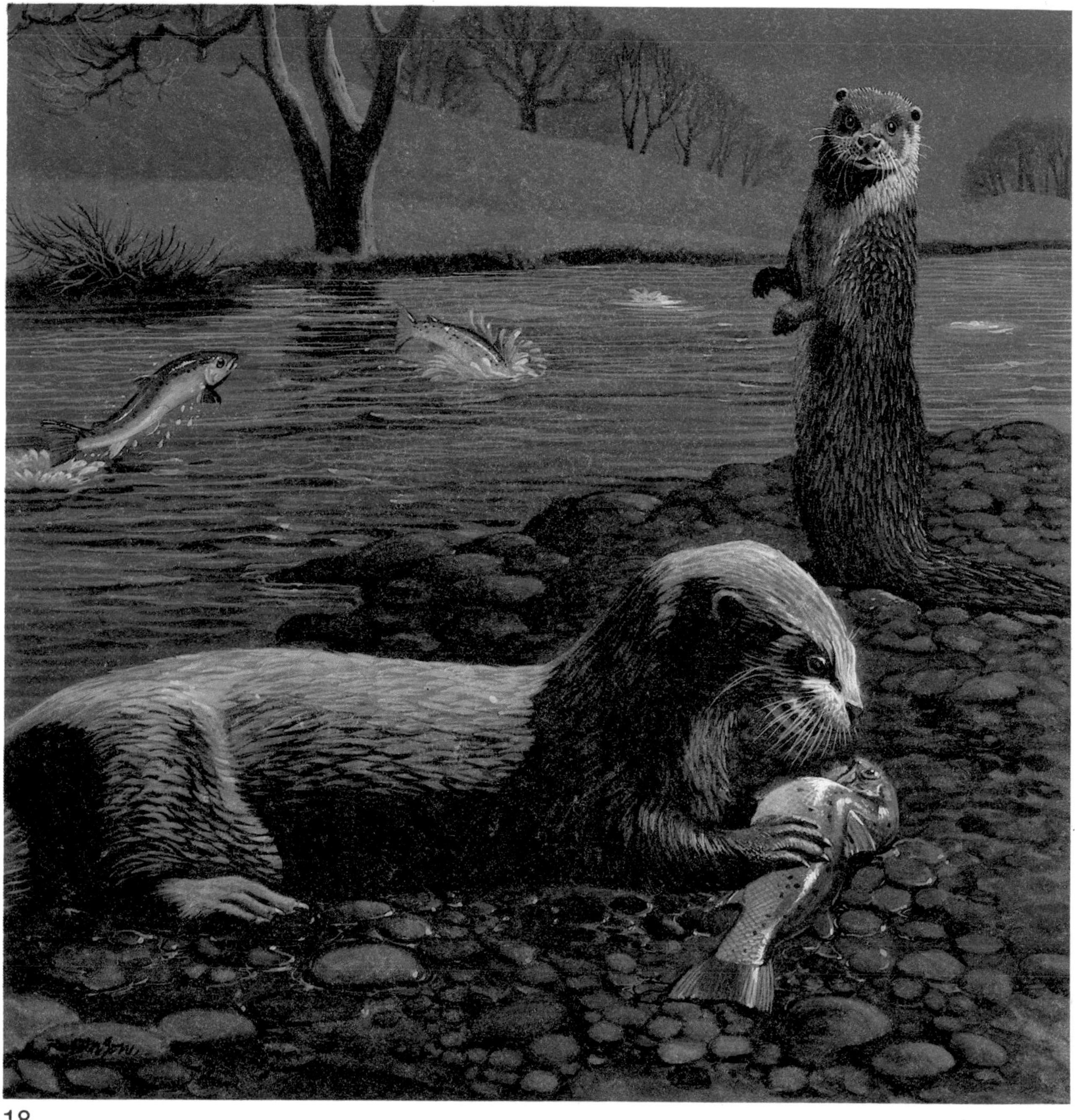

One night the otters see salmon leaping up the river. They catch one and eat it. Winter is nearly over and baby otters are growing inside the female. She leaves the river to dig a holt in a well hidden spot. When the cubs are born she feeds them with her milk and sometimes her mate brings food for her.

For eight weeks the otter looks after her cubs in the snug tunnel. Then one night she pushes them out of the entrance and sets off for the river. The young cubs are frightened as they watch their mother trot away, down to the river bank. Then, one by one, they run after her into a strange new world of sky, wind and water.

The otter dives into the water then climbs out again. Gently she pushes her young cubs to the edge. One cub slips, but its frightened squeaks stop when it feels the warm smooth water on its back.

Soon all the cubs are diving, splashing and
swimming. One climbs onto its mother's back for a
ride. She shows them how to catch fish and shellfish
in the river. All through spring the young otters
explore the river bank, finding things to eat.

Soon after the cubs were born, the male otter left
and swam downstream on his own. The growing
cubs will soon leave their mother too, but next
winter she will find a new mate and have more cubs.

More About Otters

There are two types of otter – river otters and sea otters. The otter in this story is a river otter. Sea otters are shorter and fatter than river otters. They live, breed, eat and even sleep in the sea. Otters are perfectly suited for their life in the water. They can swim very fast and with their long slim bodies they find it easy to roll over and to turn in small circles.

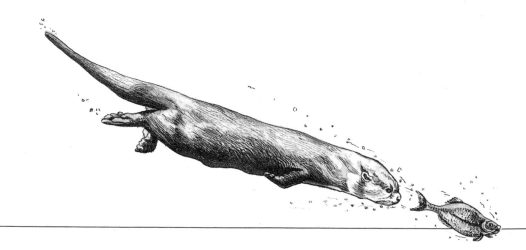

The largest otters live in South America and sometimes grow as long as a tall human. European otters are about half this size, and the smallest otters, which live in Asia, are about the same size as a large cat.

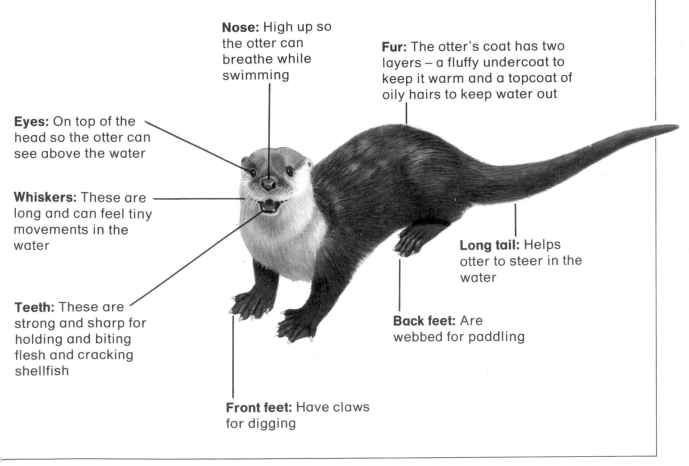

Nose: High up so the otter can breathe while swimming

Fur: The otter's coat has two layers – a fluffy undercoat to keep it warm and a topcoat of oily hairs to keep water out

Eyes: On top of the head so the otter can see above the water

Whiskers: These are long and can feel tiny movements in the water

Long tail: Helps otter to steer in the water

Teeth: These are strong and sharp for holding and biting flesh and cracking shellfish

Back feet: Are webbed for paddling

Front feet: Have claws for digging